My Proper Tea

…the journey, the stories,

and the infusion of the heart…

Central Region of Florida

Brenda Santelises

Apollo Beach, Florida, U.S.A.

Entire Contents Copyright © 2007 Red Key Internacional, LLC
& the:

a division of RED Key Internacional, LLC

My Proper Tea
...the journey, the stories & the infusion of the heart...
By Brenda Santelises, CIPS, CSP, NCP, TRC
www.TheEtiquetteDiva.com
1.800.KEY.1240
Brenda@Santelises.com
Printed in the United States of America by Lulu, Inc.

Library of Congress Cataloging-in-Publication Data available
upon request.

ISBN 13: 978-0-6151-8248-3

Table of Contents

Preface

What started as an easy "review of tea rooms" project turned into an experience that I could not possibly refuse to share. As a certified Etiquette consultant, I wanted to take on superior "tea knowledge" – I wanted to visit all the different tea rooms, and learn more about the many varieties and rituals my readings of tea explored. I wanted to know what "the big deal" is behind that magical tea time celebrated at such places like The Grand Floridian Resort at Walt Disney World®.

As I started to schedule tea time, I expected a collage of menus and teas – nothing more. Was I in for a surprise! Tea time means, to many, a journey away from the anxieties of everyday life, and a reflection on a moment that is unhurried and should be meditated upon. For others, it was necessary to take me on the same path that would lead them to tea room ownership. We shared tears, laughs, and wow's – but most of all, we shared our hearts. I shared the reasons that prompted me to write about my "Tea Experiences"; they shared their human touch and connection of unforgettable service with and for others.

For the tea lover in you, may you enjoy discovering a new tea room to call your favorite, may you cherish the stories behind each tea cup served, and may you appreciate the delight and elegance of the actual moment...

Because I have visited each and every tea room selected, I can only guarantee that each of your experiences will have a different relationship with your preferences and desires – it should! However, I can promise that each one has the potential to teach you something new and to be grateful for the many gifts that you do have, as well as the ones others are willing to share with you...

Enjoy many "cuppas" sure to infuse your own heart!

Brenda Santelises
"The Etiquette Diva"

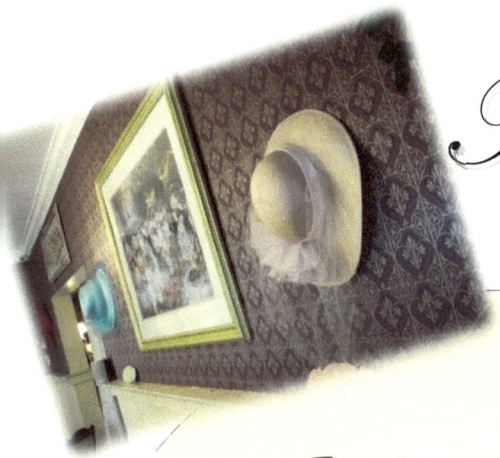

Acknowledgements

Thank you to each and every tea room who allowed me to manifest my passion for research and writing while enjoying fantastic service and one perfect cup of tea after another!

Thank you to the tea room who allowed me to put on an apron and dive right into your kitchen, watch an orchestrated cooking operation, and serve your guests by your side. What an honor! Your service is first class and no other opportunity could have been more perfect!

Thank you to Yolanda Vazquez-Fugit for sharing tea time with me, even if in the most challenging circumstances! Your patience and Great Spirit were a must that day, and you certainly kicked it in gear when needed most!

Thank you to all of you who keep asking, "Well, is it done yet?" Now it is! Cherish and enjoy every minute of it with an aromatic cup of tea! I did...

The

NOW OPEN

The Magnolia
Tea Room & Gift Shop
FOR RESERVATIONS CALL

212 Howard Street
Auburndale, FL
☎ 863.965.1684
Mon ~ Sat
11 - 3
MagnoliaTea
RoomAndGiftShop.com

My Proper Tea Experience:

*Holiday Tea – Citrus, Cinnamon,
Almond, Clove
*Apple & Prosciutto Croissant
*Butternut Squash Soup
*Lemon Cranberry Scones
*Clotted Cream- Cream Cheese Base

Magnolia

Tea Room & Gift Shop

A scenic drive full of water views – a mere 12 minutes from Interstate 4, with a promising delight of a quaint historic downtown era, preserved just right to warrant a feel of yesteryears. This is exactly what Tabitha Hill, now owner of "The Magnolia", experienced when had her baby shower five years ago at this very same 1908 built Victorian retreat. This experience stayed with her, so it came to no surprise when she asked her husband "will you buy me the tea room?" – Which she noticed for sale in 2005 as she drove towards her prenatal check up for their second little girl! Proudly, Tabitha tells how timely this venture has been, as owning this tea room has allowed her to remain a "stay at home mom". Yep – the family now lives right upstairs of a home and business they managed to remodel in just under 4 weeks!

The Magnolia Tea Room is easy to find, nestled in one of the town's corner, visible from its Main Street. A very large parking lot is just adjacent and on the same property, with a trellis canopy welcoming your visit to pass just through its bench filled portico and through the home's main door into the receiving gift shop. Just to the right, once inside, you can't miss the gentleman's tailored tea tables – with just the right mix of darker hues and perfect amount of seasonal décor. Once past this receiving area, there are three separate rooms, for a total capacity of approximately 50 tea lovers. One room in particular is set aside and available for private gatherings, inclusive of private arched entry, tea time clothing props, and in a happy pale yellow palette. The main room features a fireplace and all chairs are cushioned in fabric, with white linen napkins as a final elegant touch…

HIGHLIGHT – Petite Crunchy & Soft Center Scones

Trish's

a tea, trinket & treasure boutique

*N*ew certainly has its perks! Trish's teas will transport you to what seems like a "make believe" town – a new trend of self serving neighborhoods, with neotraditional facades, yet a new crisp line-up of "shops around the corner" ready to meet your every need! Pat Jones-Petrick, the tea room's owner had envisioned finding just the perfect corner – as is, adjacent to this downtown's fountain and park where monthly movies are featured – after 3 years of searching for the one tea room to call her own. Pat is no stranger to the tea business, modestly selling teas online, while establishing relationships with the finest tea purveyors around the world for the last 4 ½ years.

What made my eyes glow? The fantastic variety of loose leaf teas – over 150 available to indulge during your visit, and over 100 "to go" in 2, 4, or 8 oz. sizes! Do you enjoy being in "Candyland"? Well, you will feel there here too! Trish's offers chocolate and candy covered spoons to flavor your teas to your heart's content, as well as its own White Chocolate Lavender scone mix! Are you tempted now?

More perks…Free wi-fi internet, and two separate tea salons allowing for lively private events adjacent to the decorative pastel covered cabinetry backdrops, and a working piano. Have kids? Bring them in for Teddy Bear tea – which awards kids (boys & girls) with a purple-black pirate like & similar teddy bears. Speaking of awards – management at this tea room and customer service are top priority – and if you are really lucky, you may just get the whole speal, as the staff knows this tea room inside out, its history, and YES – almost every tea variety on the menu (in alphabetical order…)!

HIGHLIGHT – Purple Triple Berry Curd – Signature!

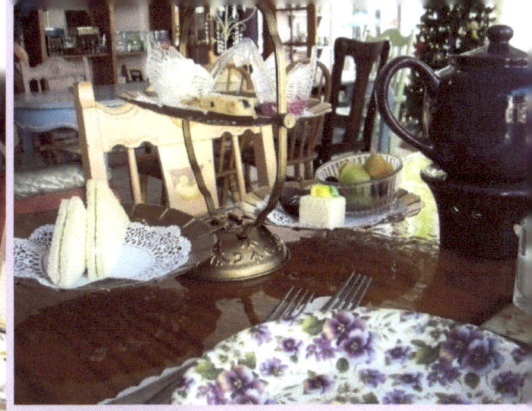

Baldwin Park Village
4844 New Broad St.
Orlando, FL
☎ **407.896.3155**
Mon ~ Sat
10 - 7
Sun 11 – 5
TrishsTeas.com

My Proper Tea Experience:

*Masala Chai – with Cream
*Mademoiselle Service – Cucumber sandwiches, Fresh fruit, Petit four & truffle
*Blueberry Scones Square
*Clotted Cream- Whip Cream Base

*T*he singing of the birdies awaits inside this tea oasis marked by a hanging tea pot & an oval shaped sign lined up with the sidewalk off the main street. At one of the most convenient and easy to find locations, Victorian Grace opts to create a natural ambiance where customer satisfaction and the greatness of a good meal are most important. Now owned by Geeta Sue-Wah-Sing and Lorraine Paul, you are still served by Grace – who now manages the tea room, and who the tea room is named after.

Since 2002, this tea room has taken over the entire transformed 1960's home, allowing for lots of room – yet several private tea areas ideal for smaller and secluded gatherings. Geeta started visiting this tea room in 2004, and when Grace was good and ready to sell (to enjoy and "smell the tea"), Geeta and her partner anxiously took over in September of 2006.

Lots of linens are used throughout, inclusive of fresh hand towels in the whimsical washroom. Although the ambiance is rather elegant and girly girl like, Victorian Grace does not seem to have a challenge attracting the male visitors, who enjoy the fresh soup offerings made right in the tea room's kitchen.

Speaking of menu, the only fixed items are the Chicken Salad and Cucumber sandwiches, as your hostesses like to add on a daily element of surprise for all other offerings. The scones seem to be a favorite in the area – which patrons claim to be "the best they have ever had". I must say I thoroughly enjoyed their clotted cream flavoring and the unique scone flavor served during my visit!

HIGHLIGHT – Only Royal Albert private vendor – lots of variety and some discontinued exclusives! Perfect find for the teacup collector...

Grace

Tea Room & Gift Shop

My Proper Tea Experience:

*Victorian Grace Blend – secret!
*Pumpkin Soup – thinner consistency
*Chicken Salad & Cucumber Sandwiches
*Pumpkin/ Cinnamon Chip Scones
*Clotted Cream- Thick & Creamy

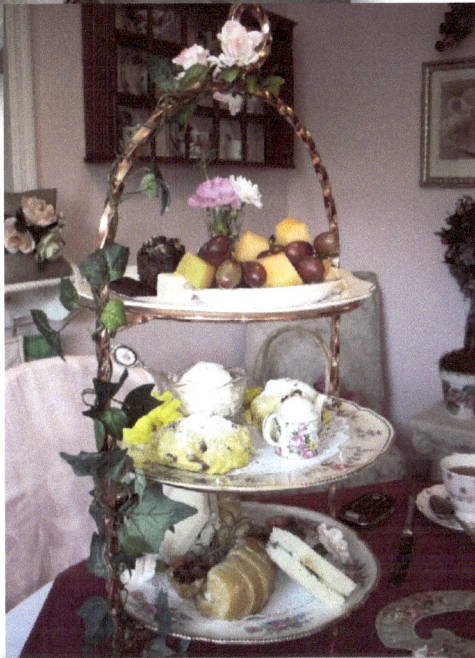

**616 N. Parsons Ave.
Brandon, FL
☎ 813.653.2662
Tue ~ Sat
10 - 4
Afternoon Tea
11, 1, 3 pm
Reservations
Preferred**

Celebration

Cagan Crossings

715 Bloom Street, Ste 130
Celebration, FL
☎ 407.566.1866
Mon ~ Thu
8:30a – 9p
Fri 8:30a – 10p
Sat 10 - 10
Sun 10 – 9
SherlocksGroup.com

My Proper Tea Experience:

*Sherlock's Classic Blend – by Harney & Sons
*Quiche Lorraine – perfect seasoning
*Plain Scone – Original & delicious!
*Clotted Cream- British Devonshire

Lake Buena Vista

Sherlock's

*J*ust look for the bright red phone booth out front and you are there! This icon is the real thing as part of British history– marked with the Queen's crown, a symbol soon to transform when the throne changes hands. All too familiar for owners Mark and Penny Thornhill – as Mark was a guard at Buckingham Palace during Princess Diana's time!

I visited their Celebration location – a perfect site just adjacent to the Celebration Hotel where Van Morrison once stayed and borrowed one of Sherlock's tea strainers (now proudly displayed at the tea shop). The "celebrity" stories don't just end there! Mark excitedly shares his many fascinating anecdotes as he points to countless pictures of him with such legends as Elton John and Eric Clapton, and even the Queen and Prince Charles. He also takes pride in the displays of Paul Burrell's teapots & wines; Paul being a regular at this tea room and Mark's very good friend who now lives in Celebration. Paul also can share a story or two of his many years as one of Princess Diana's butlers.

I would call this location "rubbing shoulders" with the locals, as its size is just precise for a couple tables indoors with an extra outdoor patio with additional seating under a canopy. Both the indoors and outdoors are under renovation to further assimilate the upgrades of the two updated new locations at Cagan Crossings in Clermont & Lake Buena Vista.

This tea room is very casual - certainly a conversation piece - however, do expect a true British loose leaf infusion in modernized "Forlife" teapots, fresh baked scones & cookies accompanied by true Devonshire cream. There are no additives to any of their menu items & some are sugar free. Their complete menu is online.

HIGHLIGHT – Champagne Afternoon Tea– Sherlock Holmes Tea

9

Infusion Tea

A mystifying vision started "InfusionTea" in trendy College Park in Orlando, as spouses Christina & Brad Cowherd studied how to cook healthier for children during their Peace Corps tour in Guatemala from 2002 to 2004. Their learning gave them enough cravings to open a place by December 2004; where tea meets a 60% organic menu with 3 Vegan offerings; as well as time for art, poetry, live music, and Chinese medicine workshops...

About a third of their space is devoted to retail with individual booths leased by separate local artists who also dedicate floor time in accordance to an agreed rotating schedule.

Infusion Tea is a very busy spot for a crowd aging anywhere between the young and the young at heart (including a 92 year old local pianist!) You walk just past an outdoor sitting area covered by large umbrellas, frequented by those appreciative of the drive by view & free Wi-fi service. As you step into the main lobby, you witness a bar where many line up for quick take out service or place an order to sit with an assigned number, at one of the lime green Ikea brand tables. Just behind the bar, the teas are displayed in jumbo clear glass canisters – a pretty impressive sight. This large store sits approximately 75 tea lovers.

The menu is extensive with over 70 tea varieties, including Yerba Mate and other organic drink specialties – Eggnog Latte, Coconut Crème Latte, and Powershots of Organic herb. Lunchtime is always a crowd favorite, with Gazpacho Soup and Banana Bread at the top of the list – both organic Peace Corps recipes.

HIGHLIGHT – Tea infused in front of your eyes in your own contemporary see through glass oversized tea cup. What an eye pleaser!

free wireless internet

Back Porch

My Proper Tea Experience:

*Kashmiri Chai – "Cha-Cha Chai" (latte)
*Caramel Crème Brulee – Bin 192
*KiwiBerry Coconut – Bin 183
*Blueberry & Ginger Peach Scones
*Shortbread Cookies – Chocolate & Butter

**639 N. Citrus Avenue
Crystal River, FL
☎ 352.564.1500
Low Season – Summer/
Early Fall
High Season – Nov – May
Call for Hours
BackPorchGarden.com**

Garden
& Tea Bar

What happens on the porch...Stays on the porch!

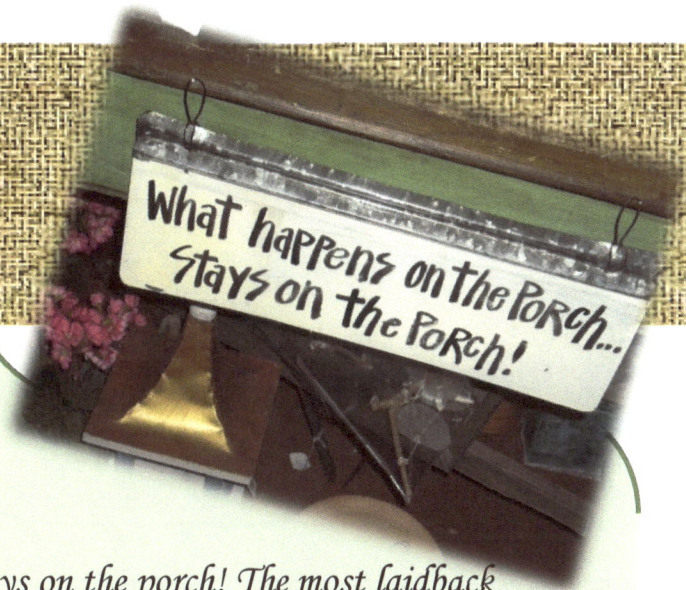

What happens on the porch...Stays on the porch! The most laidback attitude created subconsciously by a couple whose passion is to simply breath and live health, as well as be in balance with peaceful harmony. What a perfect place to be — a place where fishermen and their mates abound seasonally to enjoy the natural habitat of manatees and other sea life, amidst a friendly population of just over 3800.

I felt as though Gail & Norman Willden had spent countless hours studying tea and its many benefits; a huge plus for those looking for great over-the-counter casual and educational conversations while taking it all in, as the Willdens have become a staple to the neighborhood and leave nothing to hide and all to share! Many locals returned during my visit, walking right through the perfectly squeaky & nostalgic mosquito screen door (the kind you would find at grandma's old ranch); with their empty galvanized tins ready for a refill out of the 50 or so imported customer's top choices & best tea in the area— all from 9-10 different plantations, no less...

Just as I sat and listened to locals chat, and asked my many questions while I continued to read the variety of displayed "garden quotes" (available for sale), Dorothy, the local "granny", walked in with warm plates of homemade blueberry & ginger peach scones. "Careful, they are warm." I was warned as I reached over and asked for one of each, which were just perfect creations that melted with each mouthful of fresh fruit incorporated into each bite!

The tea is infused right in front of your eyes by either spouse, right into a glass cup with an infuser made by "IngenueTea", as you sit embracing the over 100 year old building you are now sitting in— once the town's General Store, it's library and even a stable...

HIGHLIGHT— The BEST Chai— "Cha Cha Chai" —only 180 calories per cup!
Just like a sippable dessert—whip cream, spice powder and all...

Angel Tea Room

*L*ove…Such a short word, yet so full of power! Because of the love for beautiful teacups – the feel, artistry, and prettiness of each, collectors Brenda Tester and Margaret Angell became instant friends and now owners of the same tea room they would once visit in 1998. Strolling through the small historic town, today decorated by daily Trolley tours, Brenda & Margaret stumbled upon the "unofficial" opening of the tea room becoming its very first customers. Who would have thought such fate?

In a building dating back to 1928, and amidst a cluster of many other vibrant shops, the Angel Tea Room is approximately 10 miles off I-75 and in a town that still cherishes a great movie premiere at the local Drive-in. Dade City is also home the Citrus Packing House and Museum – once the largest citrus plant in the world! Retail at this tea room includes collectible dolls, books, stationary and Metropolitan Tea bags. Loose leaf, however, is served in the dining room along a pretty varied menu prepared by the "momma of the kitchen", Laurie.

You can't deny an instant love for this town and tea room, in pretty purple and periwinkle hues and an original and customized Angel mural symbolic of the Tea room's name. Both owners encourage an experience to be enjoyed by "everyone", catering with a smile to children and those willing to experiment and try it all! "If you don't like it, we will switch it!" says Brenda, as she reminds me, however, what they carry is a variety of familiar favorites. On a lucky day, you will find Christy – the last of the very original tea room team – serving up the delicious scones, served warm with Devonshire cream and preserves – all with love…

HIGHLIGHT- - Heart shaped scones!!! Crunchy with soft inside...

My Proper Tea Experience:

*Angel's Dream – Ceylon, blackberry & maple
*Scones of "Love"- Cranberry
*Clotted Cream – Cream cheese & sour cream base

**37847 Meridian Avenue
Dade City, FL
☎ 352.518.LOVE
Tue ~ Sat
11am-5pm
For more info:
DadeCityMainStreet.org**

15

Moffat's Cup

828 Highland Avenue
Dunedin, FL
☎ 727.776.2888
Wed – Sat
11am-5pm
MoffatsCupOfTea.com

My Proper Tea Experience:

*Citrus Blossom Tea
*Cranberry Orange Scone
*Chocolate Covered Strawberries
*Raspberry Chocolate Tarts
*Lemon Roll
*Raspberry Almond Tart
*Devonshire Cream

# of Tea

...a wee bit of Scotland!

Moffat's?, you ask? Well, the mystery is solved, transformed in an enchanting small cottage in a historic small town which actually has a high school bag pipe band! In fact, the sighting of elders in kilts sipping tea in this sister city to Stirling, Scotland is rather common. Not too long ago, Dunedin had the pleasure of the visit of a Lord who loved the ambiance of Moffat's as well as the hospitality of Ailean Lyttle-Bryant, the tea room's owner since August of 2006; whose mother's ancestors established the town of Moffat, Scotland – known for weaving and pottery.

For Ailean, the thought of a tea room was natural, as was raised under the teachings of "manners" by her mother who served a sit down dinner for the family every evening – complete with china and Irish linens. Her mother always celebrated Afternoon Tea with those of cherished companionship, cooking fresh savories – which also became an early passion for Ailean. A tribute to this upbringing is evident from the vast collections of teapots and tea cups inherited from her mother & grandmother.

At Moffat's you may enjoy seasonal creations, a "bottomless pot of tea" luncheon menu, and an afternoon tea service served at 4:00pm daily (reservations required). There are also special events celebrated, such as "Teddy Bear Parties", "Princess Parties" & "Phanthom Tea", the latter to benefit the Rhett's Syndrome Foundation.

Every item is a fresh cooked replica of mom's 50-60 year old recipes – a perfect mix for this porch hugged home nestled among mature trees and flowery landscapes – a place tea calls home...

HIGHLIGHT - Huge Chocolate Covered Strawberries! Yummm...

The Garden Gate

*T*he busiest of all tea rooms, The Garden Gate is also the largest of all tea rooms featured. I chose to drive backroads through Zellwood leading to the brick streets of downtown Mount Dora, where folks park and spend the day – shopping, dining, or simply sightseeing.

The Garden Gate is angelic, and you can't help but sigh at the detection of the budding flower pots and shop sign, in a distressed wagon just in front of the main entrance into an open courtyard where real birds sing. The entire premise consists of two separate venues, where one houses the main tea room and kitchen, and the other serves as a full blown retail store and tea room overflow. This tea room used to be the home of unwed mothers and their babies in the early 1900's. It still holds a special memory in some of the mother's and children's hearts, as some have been known to return and enjoy tea where they once lived; while re-telling their stories of struggle…

As you first stroll past the courtyard, you arrive at a receiving area where there is a sign-in book, & you are welcomed by a staff member to be seated. Reservations are highly recommended but only required for Afternoon Tea Time. It is obvious this is a favorite gathering lunch spot for many locals, but just as common is the accidental tourist who happens to curiously step in. You would be glad you did! The lunch menu is so popular, especially their salmon special, which often sells out. All at the same time, you may witness men with their significant others, a group of ladies donning their boas and hats, and children with their elders behaving just as they should… This tea room ambiance is casual enough, everyone feels right at home.

Don't forget to stop by the gift shop, where you will find everything from garden items, wedding dresses hung for display, Victorian arches, and lots of hanging details surely to get your attention…

HIGHLIGHT –Largest wedding/ special event reception area–up to 200 guests!

Tea Room

142 E. 4th Avenue
Mount Dora, FL
☎ 352.735.2158
Mon – Sat
11am-3pm
Reservations
Required for
Afternoon Tea

My Proper Tea Experience:

*Peach Tea - Iced
*Cha Cha Chai
*Chicken Salad Sandwiches
*Melon slices served on the side

10335 Cross Creek Blvd.,
Ste H
Tampa, FL
☎ 813.991.1212
Mon – Sat
10am-4:30pm
Sun – 11-4
Reserv. Recommended
ExperienceMiracles.com

My Proper Tea Experience:

*Earl Grey Loose Leaf –
Harney & Sons
*Breakfast Pita Pizza-
Deeeeelicious!

Maggie's Tea Room

"Seek the unique"

A place of reflection and inspiration, Maggie's Tea Room was named after Jackie Sayle's best friend who died of Lou Gehrig's disease just 3 months after the grand opening of the Miracles gift shop. These two gals met at a London's Theater Royal Drury Lane audition and became inseparable from that moment forward.

Maggie's can be found in a newer cluster of shops and offices in the New Tampa area, tucked away in one of the rear buildings inside the Miracles gift shop. It is a place where many blessings are shared, souls healed, and where no one is turned away. A very impressive and diverse shopping experience awaits inclusive of motivational books, new market items such as lamps and ceramics, garden items, home accents, gift and occasional items, and — of course — a variety of teapots and tea cups.

Jackie believes in "blessings" and guidance from the One above, just as the idea of retail & the tea room was a vision and concept born on a Sunday morning, returning home after church services. Jackie, alongside Real Estate colleague Teresa Rogers, dreamed a notion they would later solidify as a "feeding the community" ministry through an inspirational oasis full of encouraging books, Bibles, and unique gift items; in an English Tea Room setting!

Appreciation of those who visit is an integral part of Maggie's business plan, which incorporated a cumulative free membership VIP program that rewards patrons' purchases with coupons and special events via an email newsletter, as well as post mail. Last but not least, you must check out the Garden of Joy — a tranquil outdoor environment where tea is served and items are available for sale.

HIGHLIGHT—A fresh herb garden in rear patio, seasoning daily menu items!

The Corner Rose

"Let all you do...be done from Love" Vantrease Russell

My Proper Tea Experience:

*Angel's Dream – Dark Orange Pekoe
*Lavender Scones – SUPERB!
*Apple Cherry Scones
*Elvis Goey Cake
*Clotted Cream – Almond Flavored
*Creamy Lemon Curd
NOTE – Everything made with Splenda!!!!

510 W. Holden Avenue
Orlando, FL
☎ 407.855.8063
Mon ~ Sun
11 - 4
3 weeks a month ONLY
Reserv. Required
RussellHome.org

Tea Room

*T*here is not one minute spent at this tea room when you are not feeling more appreciative, more blessed, more thankful... As you drive through a small hidden driveway leading to the most quaint and personal tearoom available, you can't help but feel a sense of peace and wonder as to what your experience there will do for your soul. Trust you me, this tea sipping experience will touch the most intimate and humbling human emotions, as you learn this tea room's history and how it changes lives...

You will be served by one of the greatest human beings – Laura – who travels from Richland, Georgia for 3 weeks out of every month to craft a tantalizing menu, as well as serve you with genuine southern comfort and elegance. For the last week of the month, Laura returns home to spend time with family. Her service comes without a price tag – no one pays for tea service – as this gesture is left up to the tea lover to decipher an appropriate donation to benefit the adjacent Russell Home. Tea lovers have come from as far as New Zealand, although The Corner Rose does not advertise in any fashion. This fact along with hearing that for the most part, all 12 seats are reserved and booked as far out as three months, makes you understand that this place must be really special!

The Russell Home is part of Florida History, as was established in 1951 with license #1 as a non-profit home for brain damaged children by founder Vantrease "Grandma" Russell, who passed away in 2003. The first child accepted in 1951, Marilyn, is still in the home today, where she smiles, plays, and waved as I walked past one of the outdoor patios. Marilyn just turned 61 years old. The youngest of all children, Michael, is now 4 years old. Michael does not have a brain – as he was born with only a brain stem and given only weeks to live. I held his hand; I watched him eat and miraculously gleam as Janet Russell Nixon; Vantrease's daughter and now director of the Russell home; spoke to him. There are countless "children" in this home, all with their own personal story. They are all at peace. It makes me appreciate my journey...

As far as Janet, she brought the tea room "home", converting "grandma's" office into what is now the tea room – a replica of her tea room at a bed & breakfast she owned in Plains, GA, where it is said President Jimmy Carter was conceived...This was also where faith and destiny would bring Laura and Janet together!

HIGHLIGHT– Edible "Sweet Mice" treat! (See recipe section)

Pickwick's
Restaurant and Tea Room

*A*ffectionately, they call her "CeCe"- the spunky owner of the Chalet style Tea Room- known as the hometown caterer for over 25 years! Pickwick's is located in the heart of Ormond Beach in a striking stand alone building in the Trails Shopping center, an outdoor shopping experience that includes upscale retailers and boutiques such as Chico's, Anne Klein, and Talbots. The main entry is just across a huge mature and shadowing Oak Tree with a hospitable wooden coat hanger and cornered settee at reception. And although the entire shopping center and tea room are in a "facelift" process, the tea room will preserve the medieval nostalgia and reminiscent structure.

The nature of this establishment, rather busy during business lunchtime, calls for tea bag service only, presented in an elegant wooden box and including varieties from Tazo, Bigelow, and Twinings to name a few. The main focus is its menu and the fresh baked scones. Everything served is of the freshest appearance using basil, other spices and tomatoes from CeCe's garden as part of the "daily specials". You will also experience the most generous of all platters, reflective of CeCe's Greek heritage, which also influences the uniqueness in the menu. For example, the Afternoon Tea (by reservations) includes rum rice pudding as part of the many savories... Yummm!

Once inside the tea room, there are 9 tables (seating for approximately 25 people) with most, flushed right up to the glass picture windows overlooking the peaceful pond and fountain, surrounded by lots of picturesque flora. There is also an outdoor covered patio, where you can hear the natural running water sounds splashing through the fountain.

HIGHLIGHT Largest scones anywhere –Approximately the size of an entire hamburger bun! Plain flavor best served with clotted cream and preserves!

Pickwick's Tea Room

**Trails Shopping Center
262 North Nova Road
Ormond Beach, FL
☎ 386.672.1669
Mon ~ Sat
11 - 4
Reserv. Required for
Afternoon Tea**

My Proper Tea Experience:

*Raspberry Tea – Iced
*Tomato Basil Soup – FRESH Basil
*Crab Quiche – FRESH made daily
*Garden Salad – Very large bowl
*Plain Scone – HUGE
*Clotted Cream – served separately
with doily and nutmeg sprinkles
*Strawberry preserves

*I*n true Victorian fashion, you will be served at this tea room with the highest regard and elegance, while listening to instrumental background strings, among other selections. The setting is the most elaborate of all, recreating every element of relaxed tea time at its best. A personalized welcome sign awaits you, monogrammed with your first name in a display right at the entrance and again at your pre-reserved table.

The building dates back to 1919 where its purpose for existence was banking, later turning into a drug store supporting a general medical practice just above it. Many where born here – some now returning to enjoy tea and re-connect to their birthplace. These stories are such a part of the city's history, that Ellen Garrett, the tea room's owner, opted to refurbish and preserve the originally laid tile from the bank's lobby, which now is the tea room's large retail store. To enjoy the many facades of this building through the years, you may visit the gentleman's wash room and check out the wallpaper made of the many renderings of this cornered site.

As far as your experience, you will appreciate knowing that Ellen's 75 year old mother comes in every morning at 7am to cook alongside 4 or 5 other chefs who create true artistry served in the traditional English 3 tiered trays – from top to bottom, not bottom to top! Two teas of the day are selected, with a Russian teapot at main retail entry, serving daily warm samples of one of the 45 or so imported loose leaf selections.

In the tea room, each table is dressed with a glass top over tablecloths, with fresh flowers provided by the local florist. There is also a separate rounded nook area, a favorite for those just running in for a cup of tea and a quick reading of the daily news. A fireplace with Camellia details creates a meditative focus, with a large settee and two surrounding chairs facing it. Ask to also see the teapot which is the inspiration for Camellia Roses's logo used uniformly to tie in all of the customized details created by the Camellia Rose family…

HIGHLIGHT–Best for elaborate newer ambiance and layout with a dedicated Little Girl's Tea Room and menu.

Camellia Rose
Tea Room & Gifts

My Proper Tea Experience:

*Gary's Market Spice – zesty orange, cinnamon & spice
*Golden Citrus Rooibus - Caffeine-free – cinnamon, orange peel, clove
*Drop Red Gorgeous - Strawberry
*Turkey Salad Sandwich – on Marbled Pumpernickel Rye
*Expresso sorbet
*Cranberry Orange Scone

Welcome
Karen, Stephanie
and
Brenda

Camellia Rose
TEA ROOM & GIFTS

120 N. Collins Street
Plant City, FL
☎ **813.659.TCUP**
Tue ~ Sat
11, 1, 3
Reservations Please
CamelliaRose.com

27

Southern

2214 Thonotosassa Rd.
Plant City, FL
☎ 813.754.5683
Tue ~ Sat
10 - 5
High Tea Service
11, 1, 3
Reservations Please

My Proper Tea Experience:

*Peach Apricot Tea - Iced
*Cinnamon & Cream Cheese Scone
*Devonshire Cream – Vanilla Flavored
*Lemon Curd
*Plant City Strawberry Scone – a usual staple to this Tea room!

Belle's
Tea Room

With a large focus on retail of inspirational and religious books, music, boutique items and gifts, this tea room's coziness is snuggled among unique themed items in a large castle like home conveniently located just over a mile off I-4. The many collections, such as Maggi B's, Alpine Village, Land Candles, Snowbabies, I do!, and many more, have transformed this castle into the perfect place to find that perfect gift… You know, the one you can't quite put your finger on?

Rick and Susan Lewis own this tea room, which caters to the many local groups – such as Red Hat Societies – with special events and themed gatherings for all to enjoy. Susan is the most kind and hospitable who humbly admits she attends to all tea lovers personally, & sometimes sits and chats with some to share a good story. She really cares about a relaxed meditating experience, and making everyone feel as if right in their living room.

We are told that the scone recipe here is a "secret" and as well – it should be! The scones were delivered fresh and warm – shaped into autumn leaves with the yummiest vanilla flavored Devonshire cream and lemon curd.

As you walk into this tea room, you walk through arched heavy wooden doors reminiscent of medieval times – in perfect harmony to set the mood for a special tea time. You walk right into what would have been the foyer, where you immediately notice there are many separate rooms; tastefully decorated, lights dimmed, while seasonal music plays in the background.

You immediately appreciate this building's architecture – something Susan's mother would confirm, who is one of Tampa's most prominent truss engineers, recently featured as part of the "Extreme Home Makeover" team for a house transformed in nearby Tampa. Stories like this one are commonplace in a tranquil room where Susan speaks with a soothing southern accent and serves with a southern heart…

HIGHLIGHT—The largest and most extensive Retail shop of tea and gift items!

Southern Comfort
Bed & Breakfast Tea Room

*S*inging is a strength for Cathy Green, who would have never thought that it would lead to owning the Bed & Breakfast and Tea Room she owns today! As a trained nurse and teacher, Cathy has always thrived on making memories for those around her, so when time came for her and her husband Joe – a pastor and pilot – to settle into small town Ruskin, Cathy just had to excel into the right job. Delivering flowers was a perfect fit! Cathy thought "singing + flowers" to loved ones = memorable deliveries…

While delivering sympathy flowers to a wealthy businessman's widow, Cathy stumbled upon Southern Comfort. She immediately fell in love with the estate, and quickly learned that it would now be a burden to the widow. It did not take long for Cathy and Joe to realize this would become their new home.

Tea time is served only on Thursdays at 1pm - an experience mostly recommended as this place is truly a getaway – a place far from the hustle and bustle and tucked away among mature magnolia and oak trees. A plaque on the brick column out front let's you know you are home, and an extensive easy walk path to the front door is composed of recycled bricks from a demolished historic cigar factory in Ybor City, Tampa. This home was built by one of 4 of the original settlers of the town of Ruskin, which is also available for private rental for a wedding and other social events' weekend.

A personal chef from Ruskin prepares Thursday's menu, bringing fresh herbs from her garden to include in her many soups and sandwiches. Her signature is an edible Calla Lily savory which earns many compliments from visiting tea lovers. Tea bag service from Twinings, Bigelow, and Bentley varieties are currently served, with loose leaf tea soon to be incorporated.

HIGHLIGHT– Ladies Spa weekend packages including Tea time, chair massage, facial, and more…

My Proper Tea Experience:

*Earl Grey – Twinings
*Fresh flavored yogurt with wild
berries and melon
*Home-made scones served
*Devonshire Cream

Main Street

After 7 years of civil service in the Caribbean island of Cuba, the passion for helping people lingered... There had to be a way to enjoy a family affair; together; and serve others. "How people feel is what's most important", says Randi Scott, owner of the Main Street Tea House since June 2007, which was previously owned by a mother/ daughter team. It is a place where "family" has truly come together, including Randi's husband Scott, congregation members as staff, and Randi's sister as an artsy seamstress, who has dressed the staff in matching embroidered pink aprons.

Just a few steps from the Safety Harbor Resort, and on the "main street" where other small shops reside, you will find this charming tea room. You walk just under a stretched awning and past a courtyard fountain, now bearing decorative edge lighting resembling those of the finer places in the northeast, and into the retail area with contrasting wooden armoires full of tea pots and other tea lover's items. At the back wall, you will appreciate loose leaf teas displayed in medium sized labeled ceramic jars, similar to those an apothecary would display.

The ceilings are painted throughout in bluish hues, with a large sunburst highlighting a beautiful chandelier in the middle of the very open main room. Your reservation is acknowledged with your name on a ceramic plaque right at your place setting, and once seated; you can really value the many novelties that surround you. There is a lit gazebo in a corner of the room with antique chairs for sitting. Also, a nook with semi-private drapes, perfect for a party of two to relax and catch up, sitting in inviting high back thick cushioned chairs and side tables for warm teapots.

Because Randi loves to cook, all baked goodies are straight from her kitchen, but she has the most fun at the "Alice in Wonderland Tea Time", which her younger patrons claim to be a hit!

HIGHLIGHT–Hard to find maple infused sugar crystals!

My Proper Tea Experience:

*Darjeeling – Loose leaf
*Fruited Chicken Salad on croissants
*Mango Chutney Turkey rounds
*Cucumber finger sandwiches – Irish butter on Rye
*Fresh baked scones served
*Clotted Cream & preserves served

$\mathcal{Y}$ou drive through a perfectly matured tree lined street to find the Hart Sisters Tea Room, just a minute drive from the infamous Sanford waterfront! Perfect lunch and tea spot romantically tucked away at the Park Avenue Village. Once there, there is lots of greenery and trees as you drive on a pebblestone drive and parking lot. A sign off the edge of the street directs you while the open gates to the outdoor patio say "welcome"…

Inside you enjoy low light ambiance, draperies on all windows and updated plum scrolled wallpaper with Victorian white wood paneling finishes, which allows you to drift off into serenity to enjoy a Spa like experience. In fact, there is a Spa just next door, so when are you planning your next ½ day getaway? Most tables sit 2-4 tea lovers, in addition to the 2 seater Victorian bench and table perfect for a gathering of 6. (Tip - This table is rather popular – so do call ahead!)

The sisters, Anna & Susan, make a perfect team, as Anna enjoys the pans and spatulas, while Susan is the chatty entrepreneur. They started with a catering business for some of the Central Florida more elite and artistic events, which they continue to offer as an extension of their tea room kitchen. Also in the team is Susan's daughter who serves guests in elegant southern fashion, as well as her son, who is a great cook himself.

You quickly understand why the their retail store is limited and not the focus, as you experience a menu out of this world; one typically found at a sit down event or some of the finer restaurants, with seasonal soups and quiches an adventure. Their scones are very moist and in perfect flavor, and just the right size to re-order - "seconds, please"…

HIGHLIGHT –Best Tea Room luncheon–The Krabe Souffle is a must hearty have!

1305 S. Park Avenue
Sanford, FL
☎ 407.323.9448
Tue ~ Fri
11-3
Saturdays by Reservations
only!
11-4
HartSistersTeaRoom.com

Hart Sisters

Lunch Café & Tea ♡ Room

My Proper Tea Experience:

*Spiced Chai – Republic of Tea
*Krabe Souffle – a MUST try!
*House Salad – homemade
SIGNATURE dressing – Honey lemon
*Pumpkin Spices scone
*Devonshire Cream – whip/ cream
cheese blend
*Lemon Curd & Strawberry preserves
in glass cups!

A Corner of

6297 Central Avenue
St. Petersburg, FL
☎ **727.345.5353**
Mon ~ Sat
11 - 6
Sun ~ 12 – 3
Reserv. Recommended
ACornerOfEngland.com

My Proper Tea Experience:

*Holiday Blend Tea
*Green Tea Delight – my son's favorite blend
*Smoked Ham Sandwich on Wheat
*Chicken Salad Sandwich
*Bread and Butter Pudding – Yummmm (Recipe in back)

England

An Exquisite English Tea Room

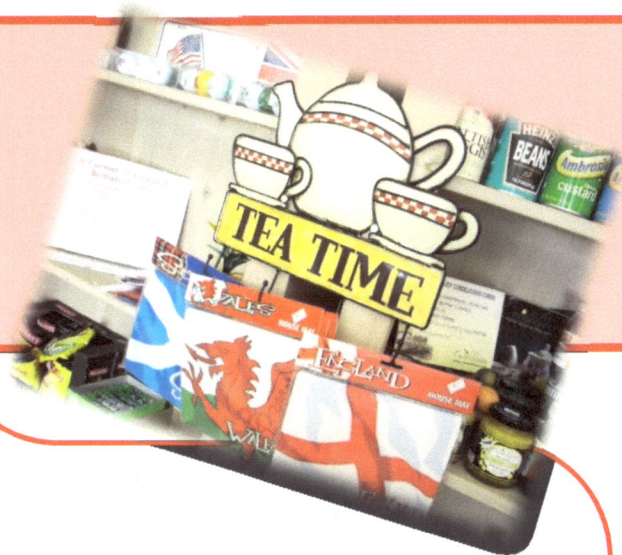

At this tea room you will have the BEST Bread and Butter Pudding you can ever imagine! This "purveyor of superior tea" is no stranger to the St. Petersburg community, as the owners, Thelma and Nazih Halawy, are now in their larger and second location. I found both to be the most humble & hospitable hosts, as they shared the many "royal" stories that are somehow attached to this tea room. For a limited time, you can get a glimpse of the red and black gown Princess Diana wore to a Spanish ball in 1985, set respectfully in a corner of the main back room of the tea room – same room that has left over wallpaper that was used in the royal London home of Queen "Mum" Elizabeth – The Clarence House situated in Pall Mall, now the official residence of Prince Charles; The Prince of Wales; and his second wife.

As you walk in, you enter a very spacious crafts and gifts shop, which also proudly offers lines of customized special occasion invitations and event goods. There are a few smaller tables set in this space just across the reception/ register area, which enjoy a brighter natural light ambiance – preferred by many locals for the quick lunch service. In the main room, there are larger tables, some arranging nicely for up to 8 tea lovers. All tables are dressed with crochet linings with many traditional tea cups and plates to admire.

Cravings for authentic English pantry products? You will find them here, as well as your favorite loose leaf teas to take home after your tea experience. You can expect a fresh special and soup of the day (including authenthically British Sheppard's Pie!)

HIGHLIGHT–Fresh tea leaves from Assam are ALL fresh flavored by Thelma in the tea room's kitchen!!!

*T*he love of a grandma, and a "labour of love" – Sofia's tea room was meant to be a jewel of the south, set in the heart of historic Tampa, and the ambiance of European elegance! For Sofia Valles, an Ybor City native & owner of this tea room, there were no second thoughts when she found the perfect tea cup set for her 4 year old granddaughter, Emily! Sofia fell in love with the ambiance and experience of tea time, as her curiosity required her to visit different tea rooms with her daughter. Before long, she took her "traveling teapot" to people's homes. An adventure lasting just over 2 years!

Friends encouraged and motivated Sofia to open what is now located caddy corner just off Henderson Avenue, in an original 1950's home, with preserved original windows and flooring creating a nostalgic ambiance reminiscent of Elvis times. In just the nick of time, an interior designer friend, a handy man building arches, and countless others provided moral support and enthusiasm; filling the space to make a dream come true...

The menu is exquisite and reflective of Sofia's Hispanic and Islander heritage, full of flavor, seasonings and soul, only shadowed by her big heart, personalized approach and smiles! Sofia enjoys catering to special evening and seasonal events – many reserved to capacity weeks before the big dates. All the teas served are loose leaf from Sri Lanka, and left warm in bottomless teapots right at your table, a service much appreciated by all who enjoy taking their time, a private moment to savor the many goodies, and having the warm cuppa as wanted, when wanted...

Your tables are draped with French toile linens, and all chairs covered with seat pads; some set in a private rear room, seating 10-12 comfortably. Amber crystal sugar, candles & tealights perfectly match the creativity and service provided by Angie & Ella who delight the many repeat guests who also enjoy the exclusive gift shop items...

HIGHLIGHT—The best and most creative fresh made desserts anywhere!

Sofia's Tea Room

& Gift Shoppe...A hidden jewel in the heart of South Tampa!

**2302 S. Hubert Avenue
Tampa, Florida
☎ 813.258.9700
Tue ~ Sat
11:30, 1:30, 3:30
Reserv. Suggested
SofiasTeaRoom.com**

My Proper Tea Experience:

*Lavender Earl Grey
*Blue Lady – Kiwi, Strawberry, Coconut – A Favorite!
*Butternut Squash Soup
*Curry Egg Salad Sandwich – Oh my, oh my!
*Curry Chicken Salad with Pistachio Sandwiches
*Othellos – Chocolate Covered Cookies with Orange liquour hint
*Pavlovas – Meringue treat with Fresh berries!

Modern Tea Time

Etiquette

The true meaning of tea time among friends lies in the essence of companionship and the enjoyment of relaxed conversation. Here are a few awareness tips of tea time etiquette.

-Follow a proper invitation; both as a hostess and as a guest. A tea time invitation should indicate more than a time and place. It should also highlight what to expect during the ceremony.

-Good quality small paper napkins are acceptable, however, a linen napkin, set folded to the left side of each place setting is preferred. The fold should have the closed edge to the left, while the open side is to the right. At a more formal tea house, the server will place the napkin on your lap.

-In order to avoid leaving your lipstick evidence on the tea cups or linen; be sure to blot your lipstick before drinking.

-If you must leave the table, place the napkin to the left of your place setting. NEVER on the chair seat! At the end, the <u>hostess</u> will place her napkin to the left of her plate to signal tea time is over.

-A hostess should always mingle and entertain with guests. If at home, she should not be stuck in the kitchen and share her "pouring" duties with appointed friends.

-Ideally, lemon slices should be thin and able to float. If using wedges instead, a small lemon fork should be provided to squeeze lemon. A cheese cloth or similar may be used. Also provide an extra saucer for discarded lemon rind. Always avoid large floating pieces, and do not dump a lemon wedge in your cup.

-Tea should always be poured first. Once so, if a buffet, guests may help themselves in an orderly fashion. If seated, wait to be served or passed the serving trays. Traditionally, there are 3 tiered platters on silver or porcelain plates. A modern serving will include savories (see "tea talk") on the bottom tray, scones on the middle tray, and sweets or pastries on the top tray.

-Always hold the tea cup by its handle. Do not "hug" the tea cup or ring your finger through the handle. You should use your index and thumb. The "pinkies up" are not necessary. Allow for a natural curved bend of your fingers instead. Again, whatever curves naturally.

-Gently swisk your tea when stirring. Do not leave your spoon in the cup and do not sip from your spoon for taste either. Always return your spoon to the saucer quietly; just behind the cup on the right hand side, behind the handle.

-If a tea bag is provided with the hot water, allow for it to rest approximately 5 minutes. Avoid "dunking" the bag, as it will not aid the process in any way. Remove the bag before drinking. A tea bag holder should be provided, otherwise, place on edge of saucer.

-If standing or seated away from table, always pick up both the tea cup and saucer.

- Tea is meant to be sipped, not slurped. Swallow all foods before sipping. Make an effort to try each course as a courtesy to your hostess. Remember that dainty bites work best, and avoid talking with your mouth full.

-When eating scones, treat as if eating a dinner roll, by breaking off in small bite sizes. Jam should be spread on first with the cream on top. Rest your used utensils on the luncheon plate – never back on the table.

-Milk is acceptable either before or after pouring tea. In early times, tea cups were made of soft paste porcelain, therefore, milk was poured BEFORE to temper the fine tea cups from cracking. Because teas differ is strength, doesn't it make more sense to pour milk after pouring and tasting? This is my preference. Enjoy!

History of Tea

Did you know that tea is the most widely consumed beverage in the world today; second only to water? Stories say that in 2700 B.C., Emperor Shen Nung, scholar and herbalist, discovered the magic of tea while sipping hot water under a wild tea tree. As he sat, a drift of leaves floated into his cup from above. He sipped, he thought, and he discovered- much like the tea drinkers of today.

Around 220 A.D., during the Han Dynasty, it was ruled that the Chinese character for tea should be pronounced "Cha" (where the word Chai derives from), followed by the invention of the Yixing teapot in 1492 A.D., made from the purple clay of Yixing, China. Now, over 500 years later, Yixing teapots are still used and preferred in China where tea drinking began!

In Europe, the first sampling of tea did not arrive until 1610 A.D., first to the Netherlands. In 1662, Charles II made tea fashionable in European high society when his bride's dowry included chests of tea. Later that century, in 1676, The English East Tea Company imports tea of its own; while in 1700, Chinese Tea became the first internationally traded commodity.

In the meantime, Russia had been enjoying tea since 1618, when the first tea reached Russia as a gift from the Chinese to Tsar Alexis. Tea was very much a cherished commodity, as it took up to 18 months for tea to travel from China to Russia; until the completion of the Trans-Siberian Railway in 1903, which minimized travel time to one week.

The first London Tea Room is recorded to have opened in 1804 – the same city to take the credit for the three course afternoon tea time, sometime in 1901-1914.

Stateside also plays a historical role, with the imposing of tea tax as an Act of Parliament in 1767. A tax was imposed on all tea shipped by the East India Company to the American colonies. Then in 1773, a band of Boston men, disguised as Native Americans, boarded the ship Dartmouth and threw 340 chests of tea overboard. The British government's closure of Boston Harbor and the arrival of British troops on American soil started the historic War of Independence... This event is known as the Boston Tea Party.

Paraphrased from – *Tea Time World Wide©*

Types of Tea

Did you know that all true tea comes from the Camellia sinensis plant? Yep! The different types stem from its processing, with 3 main varieties: black, oolong, and green. Let's take a look:

BLACK - oxidized and fermented during processing, to give them their distinctive flavours. Black tea has a full, rich taste.

-KEEMUN - considered by most to be the finest of all Chinese black teas. It's smooth and very aromatic.

-DARJEELING - Named for the Darjeeling province in India, this fine black tea is another worth trying. The Darjeeling region also produces excellent green and oolong teas.

-LAPSANG OUCHONG - Another black tea from China, this tea has a strong smoky flavour that many find delicious.

-ASSAM - A very full-bodied tea, but without the hint of spice found in Keemun. It's grown in northern regions of India. The flavour is strong and rich, and great with breakfast.

-EARL GREY - plain black tea, infused with the citrus flavour of bergamot (similar to orange blossoms). This gives a bright, tart and refreshing tea that is unlike other black teas.

OOLONG - it falls between a black and a green tea. It only undergoes a small amount of fermentation during processing.

GREEN - have undergone less processing than black teas, and have a much lighter flavour. The health benefits of green tea are seemingly endless. Since the leaves are not fermented, the taste is pleasantly fresh and herbal.

-SENCHA - the most popular of Japan's green teas. It has a lightly astringent taste along with a slight sweetness.

-DRAGON WELL - (also called Lung Ching) is the ultimate green tea. The colour is bright green and the flavour is quite brisk. Be prepared to pay more than usual for this quality tea.

-GUNPOWDER - These tea leaves are rolled into tight, little balls that apparently resemble old-style gunpowder. Because of the rolled form, Gunpowder tea stays fresher longer than most other green teas. The taste is fresh and a little grassy.

-JASMINE - Jasmine isn't exactly a kind of green tea, but is a blended tea with green tea leaves and jasmine flowers. The blossoms give the tea a very refreshing taste, and fragrant aroma.

WHITE - Just like those other teas, it comes from the Camellia sinensis plant. But the leaves are picked and harvested before the leaves open fully, when the buds are still covered by fine white hair. Hence the name. White tea is scarcer than the other traditional teas, and quite a bit more expensive.

ROOIBOS - Not a true tea! The Rooibos plant is a small shrubby bush that only grows in South Africa. Rooibos tea is a distinctive red colour and its taste is also unique with a very sweet and slightly nutty flavour. Its delicious taste and numerous healthful qualities have helped Rooibos become a popular tea all over the world.

Source: Sean Paajanen – Coffee/Tea – *About, Inc.* ©

Tea Talk

Simple & common phrases and terms in the tea world, for the tea novice…

- *Afternoon Tea – usually in late afternoon and also referred as "low tea", as usually next to low tables, such as coffee tables. There are three basic types of afternoon teas:*
  - *Cream - Tea, scones, jam and cream*
  - *Light - Tea, scones and sweets*
  - *Full - Tea, savories, scones, sweets and dessert*
- *Aroma - Smell or scent denoting 'inherent character' usually in tea grown at high altitudes.*
- *Bergamot - The essential oil of the bergamot orange, which is mixed with black tea to give Earl Grey tea its characteristic flavor.*
- *Blend - A combination of different types of teas for flavor consistency from season to season.*
- *Brisk - The most 'live' characteristic. Results from good manufacture.*
- *Ceylon – Teas from Sri Lanka.*
- *Cha - Romanized spelling of the Chinese and Japanese characters for tea.*

- *Chai - pronounced as a single syllable that rhymes with "pie", is a spiced milk tea with most commonly cardamom, cinnamon, ginger, cloves, and pepper.*

- *Curd - is a dairy product obtained by curdling (coagulating) milk with rennet or an edible acidic substance such as lemon juice (lemon curd most common).*

- *Devonshire Cream - Originally from Devonshire County, England, it is a thick, buttery cream often used as a topping for scones.*

- *Fannings - Leaf particles that have been sifted out of high quality teas.*

- *Formosa - Tea produced in Taiwan; primarily Oolong teas.*

- *High Tea - in all actuality, high tea, or "meat tea" is dinner. It is served later (usually after 6pm), and there would also be meats, fish or eggs, cheese, bread and butter, and cake. It is more of a man's meal, than a ladies social diversion.*

- *Infusion – the act of introducing one substance into another, os as to change its very essence.*

- *Muscatel - Desirable character in Darjeeling teas. A grape taste.*

- Orange Pekoe - A grade of large, whole leaf tea; does not describe flavor.

- Pastries - Cakes, cookies, shortbread and sweets.

- Pekoe - A grade of small, whole leaf tea, from the Chinese term baihao, which refers to the white hairs of the new buds on the tea plant.

- Polyphenols - Astringent compounds found in tea.

- Savories - Tiny sandwiches or appetizers.

- Scones - The scone is a British snack of Scottish origin. A small quickbread made of wheat, barley or oatmeal, usually with baking powder as a leavening agent.

- Theine - A synonym for caffeine.

- Tisane - Herbal tea, that is teas produced from the leaves of plants other than the tea plant.

Recipes...

Herbed Cream Cheese Tea Sandwich

1 8oz pkg organic cream cheese, softened
1 Tbsp dried cranberries
1 Tbsp toasted walnuts, chopped
1 Tsp parsley, dried
½ Tsp freshly dried ground pepper

Mix all ingredients. Serve on organic fruit & nut bread.

Courtesy of Infusion Tea

Chocolate Cream

4 oz softened cream cheese
¼ C heavy whipping cream
1/8 C of your favorite chocolate syrup

Mix cream cheese with mixer until creamy, add heavy whipping cream and mix until well combined and creamy, add chocolate syrup and mix slowly until combined.

Courtesy of Hart Sisters Tea Room

Chocolate Chip Scones

2 C All Purpose flour
2/3 C Granulated Sugar
1 ½ Tsp Baking Powder
¾ Tsp Baking Soda
¼ Tsp Salt
½ C Cold Butter cut up in pieces
½ C Semi Sweet Chocolate Chips
2/3 C Sour Cream
1 Egg slightly beaten

Preheat oven to 425 degrees. Blend flour, sugar, baking powder, baking soda & salt until well combined. Work the butter in with your fingers until about the size of peas. Stir in the chocolate chips. Make a well in the center & add the sour cream and egg mix until just blended. Turn out onto a floured board. Pat gently into a circle to about ½ to ¾ of an inch thick. Cut into triangles with a floured knife. Place on a lightly greased pan. Bake at 425 for 14 to 16 minutes or until lightly golden.

Courtesy of Hart Sisters Tea Room

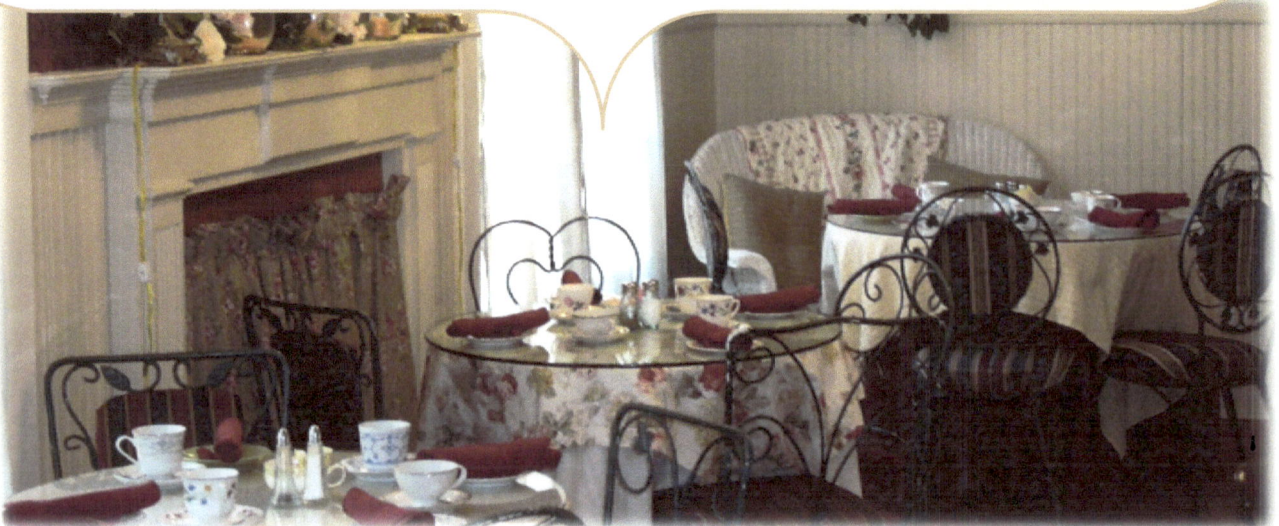

Almond Flavored Clotted Cream

1 C heavy whipping cream
¼ C powdered Sugar
1 Tsp almond flavor

Beat on HIGH in mixer until thickened.

Courtesy of The Corner Rose Tea Room

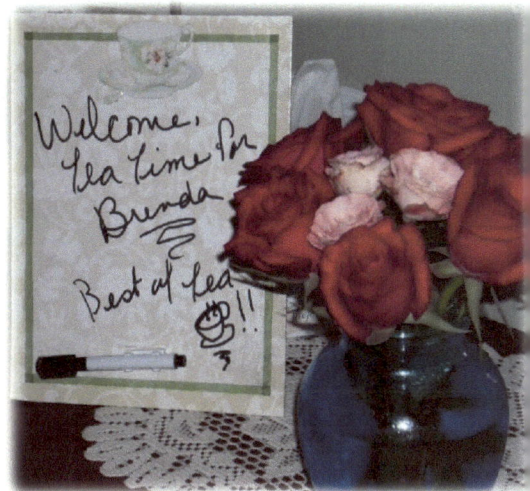

Sweet Mice

Maraschino cherries with stems
Chocolate Almond Bark or Melting Discs
Sliced almonds with brown trim
Hershey's kisses
Small tube of white icing for eyes

Melt chocolate in microwave safe cup. Add Tsp of oil if too thick. Drain cherries of all liquids. Dip cherries in melted chocolate & place on wax paper. Let set a minute. Dip bottom of kisses in melted chocolate. Attach to cherries and let sit. Set almonds in place as ears and squeeze small dots of white icing as eyes.

Courtesy of The Corner Rose Tea Room

Bread and Butter Pudding

3 oz Raisins
¼ C Amaretto liquor
12 slices white bread, crusts removed
1 ½ stick unsalted butter, melted
9 egg yolks
2 Tsp vanilla paste
¾ C sugar
½ C milk
2 C heavy cream
2 Tbsp granulated sugar to dust top of pudding
3 oz sliced almonds, lightly toasted
2 Tbsp powdered sugar

PRINCESS DIANA'S FAVORITE!

Soak raisins in Amaretto and cover at room temperature 6-8 hrs. Preheat oven to 350. Cut 4 slices of bread into ½ inch dice, & spread diced bread on bottom of casserole dish. Sprinkle raisins on top of bread cubes and pour any remaining Amaretto over bread. Cut remaining slices in 4 even triangles. Dip triangles into butter and arrange atop raisins, overlapping triangles slightly. Pour remaining butter over bread. Whish yolks, vanilla paste and sugar in large bowl until combined. Bring milk and cream to boil in high heat. Pour hot mix onto egg yolks whisking constantly. Pour warm egg mixture over bread and let soak for about 20 minutes. Place casserole dish in roasting tray filled halfway with water and bake for 30-45 minutes.
Sprinkle with extra sugar and broil or torch to caramelize sugars. Sprinkle with toasted sliced almonds and dust with powder sugar.

Courtesy of A Corner of England

Reuben Soup

Beef broth base
Sautee Onions and butter to taste
Add Saur Kraut
Add flour to thicken to taste
Stir to not gain "flavor nuggets"
Simmer for a "while"
Add shredded corned beef and smokey swiss
Stir in Heavy Cream & Sherry wine
"Throw in" chopped marble rye bread

Done!

Courtesy of Tussie Mussie's Tea Room

Diabetic Orange Cake

1/3 C reduced calorie margarine, melted
1/4 C granulated brown sugar substitute
1 Tsp powdered sugar substitute
1 egg
1 ¼ C flour
2 Tsp baking powder
½ Tsp baking soda
¼ Tsp cinnamon
2/3 C unsweetened orange juice
Vegetable cooking spray

Combine margarine, sugar substitutes and egg. Beat at high speed with an electric mixer for 2 minutes. Combine flour, baking powder, soda and cinnamon, stirring to blend. Add flour mixture to creamed mixture alternately with orange juice, beginning and ending with the flour. Beat at low speed after each addition. Spoon batter into an 8 inch square pan coated with cooking spray. Bake at 350 degrees for 25-30 minutes or until a toothpick comes out clean when inserted. Note: You can make two of these and layer them if you wish or bake them in round pans instead. 9 servings.

118 calories, 19 grams carbo, 3 gm protein, 3 gm fat, 257 mg sodium, 30 mg cholesterol.

Source – Seeds of Knowledge©, by Brenda Hyde

Easy Cranberry Scones

1 ½ C flour
1/3 C sugar
2 Tsp baking powder
½ Tsp salt
¾ C heavy cream
2 Tsp finely shredded lemon zest
½ C dried cranberries

Preheat oven to 375. Mix together the flour, cranberries, sugar, baking powder, and salt. Make a well in the center and and pour in the cream and lemon peel. Stir together until crumbly then use your hands to gently knead the dough into a ball.

Place ball onto floured surface and either roll out or pat the dough into a circle (7 1/2" around). Cut the dough like pizza into 6 - 8 wedges.

Place scones 1" apart on an ungreased cookie sheet. Lightly brush scones with additional cream and sprinkle with sugar if you like. Bake about 18 minutes or until scones are golden brown. Serve warm.

Source – Seeds of Knowledge©, by Lisa Worrell

Sweet Potato Pie Soup

2 Tbsp (1/4 stick) butter
1 C chopped onion
2 small celery stalks, chopped
1 medium leek, sliced (white and pale green parts only)
1 large garlic clove, chopped
1 ½ pounds red-skinned sweet potatoes (yams), peeled, cut   into 1-inch pieces (about 5 cups)
4 C chicken stock or canned low-salt chicken broth   (use vegetable broth for vegetarian option)
1 cinnamon stick
1/4 teaspoon ground nutmeg
1 ½ C half and half
2 Tbsp maple syrup
pinch brown sugar
Miniature Marshmallows
The leafy tops of the celery stalks, chopped

Melt butter in a large, heavy-bottomed pot over medium-high heat. Add chopped onions & sauté for about 5 mins. Add chopped celery stalks & leek, sauté about 5 mins. Add garlic and sauté 2 mins. Add sweet potatoes, chicken stock, cinnamon stick, brown sugar, & nutmeg; bring to boil. Reduce heat & simmer uncovered until potatoes are tender, about 20 minutes. Remove cinnamon stick & discard. Working in batches, puree soup in blender. Return to pot. Add half & half and maple syrup and stir over medium-low heat to heat through. Serve sprinkled with marshmallows & celery leaves.

From My Kitchen…With love!